JAPANESE MYTHOLOGY

Dragons of Japanese Mythology

BY KARI CORNELL

CONTENT CONSULTANT
WAKAKO SUZUKI, PhD
ASSOCIATE PROFESSOR OF ASIAN AND MIDDLE EASTERN STUDIES
WHITMAN COLLEGE

Kids Core
An Imprint of Abdo Publishing
abdobooks.com

abdobooks.com

Published by Abdo Publishing, a division of ABDO, PO Box 398166, Minneapolis, Minnesota 55439.

Printed in the United States of America, North Mankato, Minnesota.
102024
012025

Cover Photo: Shutterstock Images
Interior Photo: The History Collection/Alamy, 4–5, 28 (left); Shutterstock Images, 6, 14–15, 22–23, 29 (top); Artokoloro/Penta Springs Limited/Alamy, 9; Warwick Goble and Grace James/Album/British Library/Alamy, 10; Sean Pavone/Shutterstock Images, 12; iStockphoto, 17; Utagawa Kuniyoshi/Heritage Art/Heritage Images/Hulton Archive/Getty Images, 19, 28 (right); Pictures from History/Universal Images Group/Getty Images, 20; Tawin Mukdharakosa/Shutterstock Images, 24, 29 (bottom); Paul Polydorou/Bridgeman Images, 26

Editor: Christa Kelly
Series Designer: Ryan Gale

Library of Congress Control Number: 2024938397

Publisher's Cataloging-in-Publication Data

Names: Cornell, Kari, author.
Title: Dragons of Japanese Mythology / by Kari Cornell
Description: Minneapolis, Minnesota: ABDO Publishing, 2025 | Series: Japanese mythology | Includes online resources and index.
Identifiers: ISBN 9781098295943 (lib. bdg.) | ISBN 9798384916949 (ebook)
Subjects: LCSH: Mythology, Japanese--Juvenile literature. | Deities--Juvenile literature. | Dragons--Juvenile literature. | Dragons--Folklore--Juvenile literature. | Mythology, Asian--Juvenile literature.
Classification: DDC 398.21--dc23

CONTENTS

Ryujin is also called Watatsumi.

CHAPTER 1

The Jellyfish and the Monkey

In Japan's earliest days, a dragon king ruled the sea and all its creatures. The dragon's name was Ryujin. He lived at the bottom of the ocean in a beautiful palace. It had walls made of coral.

In some stories, Ryujin is kind. In others, he is dangerous.

The ceiling was made of jade stone. The garden had trees of pink, red, and white coral.

But even with all his riches, Ryujin was unhappy. He was lonely. He wanted a wife.

Ryujin asked a school of fish to find him a dragon to marry.

The fish arrived back at the palace with a beautiful young dragon. She had green scales that sparkled in the light. Her eyes shone like fire. She wore flowing robes decorated with jewels. The king fell in love instantly. The dragons married and had a big party. All the creatures of the sea came to wish them well.

The Dragon's Pearl

Some people believe dragons have a pearl that gives them their power. In some stories, Ryujin has a pearl that can make people live forever. He carries the pearl in his forehead.

Ryujin and the dragon queen were happy. Then disaster struck. The dragon queen got very sick. Ryujin called for a doctor. The doctor gave the queen medicines. None of them worked.

Finally, the doctor decided the only cure was eating a monkey **liver**. Ryujin did not know what to do. How could he get a monkey liver? Monkeys lived on land.

Suddenly, the dragon king's assistant had an idea. Jellyfish had four legs and a shell. They could walk on land. The king could send a jellyfish to capture a monkey!

Ryujin sent a jellyfish to an island where many monkeys lived. The jellyfish swam to the island and found a monkey in a tree.

According to Japanese mythology, jellyfish used to look like turtles. They were proud of being one of the few sea animals that could walk on land.

Ryujin lives in an underwater palace called Ryūgū-jō.

The jellyfish told the monkey about the dragon king's palace under the sea. He said that it was the most beautiful place in the world. The monkey asked to go see it. The jellyfish offered to take the monkey there. He told the monkey to climb on his back. Then they headed toward the palace.

Along the way, the jellyfish asked the monkey if he had remembered to bring his liver. The monkey grew suspicious. The jellyfish then told the monkey the whole story.

The monkey was scared. But he came up with a plan to trick the jellyfish. He said that he left his liver back on the island. The jellyfish had no choice but to turn around. As soon as they reached the shore, the monkey ran away.

The jellyfish swam back to the palace alone. The dragon king asked why the jellyfish had not returned with a monkey. The jellyfish shook with fear. He told Ryujin what happened.

The dragon king was furious. He ordered his servants to punish the jellyfish. It would no longer have bones. It would be flat.

Shinto is Japan's native religion. It is older than recorded history.

The servants took the jellyfish's bones. Then they tossed the creature back into the sea. No jellyfish ever had bones again.

What Is Japanese Mythology?

Japan is an island nation off the coast of Asia. People have been telling myths in Japan for thousands of years. Myths are stories. Japanese mythology is an important part of Shinto, a Japanese religion. The word *Shinto* means "way of the gods." This religion centers around *kami*, or "spirits." Some gods and monsters are kami. Animals and other parts of the natural world can be kami, too.

Many Japanese dragons are kami. They can be found in many Shinto myths. They are symbols of wealth and good fortune. Today, dragons are important parts of Japanese mythology and **culture**.

Further Evidence

Look at the website below. Does it give any new evidence to support Chapter One?

Dragons

abdocorelibrary.com/dragons-of-japanese-mythology

In Japanese, the word for dragon is *ryuu*.

The Power of the Dragon

Japanese dragons combine features from different animals. They have long, scaly, snakelike bodies. They have four legs, each with a tigerlike paw. The paws have three toes, each tipped with a sharp claw. Dragons have long, hairy heads.

Some people say their heads look like those of camels. Their ears look like those of a cow. They have deerlike antlers on the tops of their heads. Many have long whiskers.

Japanese dragons do not have wings. Instead, each dragon has a spiky crest that runs down its back. This crest helps the dragon fly.

Many Japanese dragons have special powers. They can control storms. They make clouds and bring rain. Some breathe lightning.

The First Dragon

Japanese mythology says that the first dragon began as a snake. Years later, it became a fish. Hundreds of years after that, the fish grew a tail and claws. Finally, the creature grew horns and a crest down its back.

Japanese Dragons

Most Japanese dragons share similar features.

Some Japanese dragons can shape-shift. This means they can become different animals. They can also change their size and become invisible.

Dragons of Japan

There are many dragons in Japanese mythology. One of the most famous is Ryujin. He is the king of all Japanese dragons. He is also the master of snakes. He rules the sea and all sea creatures.

Yamata no Orochi is another famous dragon. He was evil and dangerous. Yamata no Orochi had eight heads and eight tails. A forest of pine trees grew on his back. His stomach glowed red.

Ryujin has magical jewels that allow him to control the tides.

Yamata no Orochi terrorized Japan by eating a young girl every year until he was killed by Susanoo.

He could bring floods and make volcanoes erupt. The god of storms, Susanoo (pronounced soo-sah-no-oh), killed him.

Gods aren't the only ones who can kill dragons. The *karura* is a monster that eats dragons. This giant creature has a human body and a bird head. It can breathe fire. Dragons can protect themselves from this monster by carrying a special **talisman**.

Primary Source

Nguyen Ngoc Tho studies East Asian **folklore**. He describes a few Japanese dragons:

> Sui Riu is a rain-dragon . . . Han Riu is striped with nine different colors . . . Ka Riu is a small fiery red dragon . . . Ri Riu has wonderful sight . . . Fuku Riu is the Japanese Dragon of Good Luck . . . Kinryu is a golden dragon . . .

Source: Nguyen Ngoc Tho. *The Symbol of the Dragon and Ways to Shape Cultural Identities in Vietnam and Japan.* Harvard-Yenching Institute, 2015. p. 47, harvard-yenching.org. Accessed 17 Apr. 2024.

What's the Big Idea?

Read this quote carefully. What is its main idea? Explain how the main idea is supported by details.

In Buddhism, dragons are called nagas.

A Cultural Icon

The first dragons were introduced to Japan through Chinese **folklore**. In the 500s CE, Japan started to **adopt** Chinese ideas and traditions, including a religion called Buddhism. Buddhism originally comes from India.

The Kinryu no Mai festival honors Kannon, a golden dragon who came down from heaven.

Dragons are found in many Buddhist myths. They symbolize power and wisdom.

Buddhism and Shinto **influenced** each other. Dragons began to appear in many Shinto myths. **Shrines** were built to honor dragons. Farmers began to pray to dragons for rain. Dragons quickly became important to Japanese culture.

Dragons in Modern Japan

Today, dragons are easy to find in Japan. In the spring, the country holds festivals to honor Japan's dragons. At the Kinryu no Mai festival, a golden dragon dances through the streets of Tokyo, the capital of Japan. The dragon is 59 feet (18 m) long and weighs 194 pounds (88 kg). It takes eight dancers to move the dragon.

The Imperial Family

Dragons have a strong connection to Japan's imperial family. This family has ruled the country for many centuries. As a symbol of good luck, strength, and wisdom, dragons came to represent the **emperor**.

The painting on the ceiling of the Kenninji Temple was made in 2002 to celebrate the 800th anniversary of the temple.

Artwork of dragons decorates religious temples, museums, and other buildings in Japan. The dragons are often shown in the water or the clouds. In the Kenninji Temple in Kyoto, twin dragons look down from clouds on the temple's ceiling. In the town of Sakado, big dragon sculptures top the gate and roofs of the Holy Celestial Palace of 5,000 Soaring Dragons.

Japanese dragons can also be found in pop culture. They appear in several Japanese television shows, including *Dragon Ball Z* and the *Pokémon* series.

Dragons have long been honored in Japan. They bring rain and good luck. They inspire art and stories. Hundreds of years after their tales came to Japan, dragons are still treasured parts of the country's culture.

Explore Online

Read about the Kenninji Temple at the website below. Is there any information that wasn't in Chapter Three?

Kenninji Temple

abdocorelibrary.com/dragons-of-japanese-mythology

Legendary Facts

In Japanese mythology, Ryujin is a dragon king.

Dragons are important in Shinto. They are *kami*, or spirits.

Dragons can shape-shift, become invisible, and make storms.

Today, dragons are found throughout Japan.

Glossary

adopt
to take or use

culture
the beliefs and practices of a particular group of people

emperor
the ruler of an empire

folklore
myths or stories

influenced
affected

liver
an organ found in many animals

shrines
places where gods and other religious figures are honored and worshipped

talisman
an object that brings protection or good luck

Online Resources

To learn more about dragons and Japanese mythology, visit our free resource websites below.

Visit **abdocorelibrary.com** or scan this QR code for free Common Core resources for teachers and students, including vetted activities, multimedia, and booklinks, for deeper subject comprehension.

Visit **abdobooklinks.com** or scan this QR code for free additional online weblinks for further learning. These links are routinely monitored and updated to provide the most current information available.

Learn More

Bell, Samantha S. *Dragons of Chinese Mythology*. Abdo, 2023.

Hudak, Heather C. *Susanoo*. Abdo, 2025.

Yasuda, Yuri. *Japanese Myths, Legends, and Folktales: Bilingual English and Japanese Edition*. Tuttle, 2019.

Index

About the Author

Kari Cornell is an award-winning children's book author who gardens, runs, and makes pottery. She lives in Minneapolis with her husband, two boys, and their sweet dog, EmmyLou.